She Grows from Depths of Pain

Poetry and Prose

Rekha Balachandran

Chennai • Bangalore

CLEVER FOX PUBLISHING
Chennai, India

Published by CLEVER FOX PUBLISHING 2023
Copyright © Rekha Balachandran 2023

All Rights Reserved.
ISBN: 978-93-56483-92-7

This book has been published with all reasonable efforts taken to make the material error-free after the consent of the author. No part of this book shall be used, reproduced in any manner whatsoever without written permission from the author, except in the case of brief quotations embodied in critical articles and reviews.

The Author of this book is solely responsible and liable for its content including but not limited to the views, representations, descriptions, statements, information, opinions and references ["Content"]. The Content of this book shall not constitute or be construed or deemed to reflect the opinion or expression of the Publisher or Editor. Neither the Publisher nor Editor endorse or approve the Content of this book or guarantee the reliability, accuracy or completeness of the Content published herein and do not make any representations or warranties of any kind, express or implied, including but not limited to the implied warranties of merchantability, fitness for a particular purpose. The Publisher and Editor shall not be liable whatsoever for any errors, omissions, whether such errors or omissions result from negligence, accident, or any other cause or claims for loss or damages of any kind, including without limitation, indirect or consequential loss or damage arising out of use, inability to use, or about the reliability, accuracy or sufficiency of the information contained in this book.

CONTENTS

Preface .... *iv*
Acknowledgments .... *v*
Introduction .... *vi*

1. Eunoia 1
2. More or Less 14
3. Stardust Girl 39
4. For You 61
5. Mirabilia 109

PREFACE

Poetry is all about emotions. Sometimes you have to walk off the track to connect to them and when you do, they take different forms.

When I write the words become:

Moonlight in the night sky.

Ripples in the water.

The spring flowers.

The innocent smiles,

And the air which you and I breathe.

The book is beautifully illustrated with watercolor paintings and sketches so that reader would be able to connect with each poem. And in the end, I chose Whale because it symbolizes resilience, compassion, spirituality, psychic abilities, and they communicate with power of music.

It teaches you to be intuitive and find inner voice.

Rekha Balachandran

12-04-2022

ACKNOWLEDGMENTS

Love to my daughter who has always been supporting and encouraged me when I penned this book.

INTRODUCTION

The journey toward healing

Sometimes there are days when you feel lost.

Sometimes you feel empty.

It can be because of not getting a proper validation,

or it can be because you are unable to open to people around you.

There can be at times you missed your loved ones too.

It can make you confused, you tend to get anxiety,

loose sleep, don't want to watch movie, or unable to do anything.

Your daily chores can come to halt.

You need to distract and take a time off from everything.

Switch off completely from the ones you feel are spreading negativity.

Go out for a walk and do nothing, go to a restaurant,

and have your favorite food, read some books, drive alone, travel.

It will give a chance to view things from a different perspective.

And in this process, you heal.

1

Eunoia

You hold a set of keys,

To unlock you heart,

And growth is a slow process,

Seasons might come and go,

But don't rush,

Because you can't set yourself free,

If you miss a single key.

Nothing will ever be the same,

You are constantly healing,

You are constantly learning,

And constantly growing,

Sometimes it might be hard,

But it's really brave,

To constantly keep trying,

You gotta give yourself some credit.

I had lost myself somewhere,

Along the way I realized not to give up,

And reached deep down in my soul,

Found my broken wings and learned to fly.

As she went through all the chaos,

Slowly crawling and holding onto life,

Depending on whatever was keeping alive,

Shedding the layers one by one,

So that she can hide in a safe place,

A place where transformation was about to take place,

Waiting for the right time, the right moment,

One fine day only to emerging into something very, very beautiful,

And it was called metamorphosis.

Flaws of Love

Love.

Many of them have no idea.

Do you?

When you love someone, you just love them,

Through all their moods all the time,

Sometimes their worst qualities come out,

And they peak at nuisance,

As time passes their flaws becomes freckles,

But your love for them never dies.

Flaws of Love

What connects the two?

Like the yin and yang,

Like the color black and white,

Like sleep and awake,

Like weak and strong,

Like the Sun and the Moon,

Like the quiet and the loud,

Like the hot and the cold,

That's the rule of nature,

And it's a fact and it's true.

You can be madly in love,

And not be together,

Can stay miles apart,

But connected with your souls forever,

It doesn't require physical connection,

Always remember souls are connected,

Through the energy of two spirits,

That's why they are called soulmates.

There are people who might come into your life,

They come with different lessons,

Some might teach you how to grow,

Some might teach you how to love,

Some might show you what's the importance of you, just like a mirror.

There's always that one person in this world,

Who would love you no matter who you are,

No matter how broken you are,

No matter how imperfect you are,

And that's what matters the most,

Because you are never judged,

And you are loved more with each passing day.

Selfless Love

Let every atom in the body,

love you like no one has ever.

Because even though you might be broken,

there so much to be done.

And all those broken parts must be healed,

because the story is yet to be written.

Selfless Love

2

More or Less

She had a feeling like never before,

As if the wilderness was calling her,

Or it was all in her head,

A voice never heard before,

It was a never-ending thirst,

To embark on a journey and,

a quest to find unanswered questions.

How we met is an interesting tale,

From the moment we, we knew,

We were going to stay together forever,

Unlike any other fairytale.

Home

That day something was different,

my mind and heart were sleeping,

as if the nature was trying to warn me,

something was gonna change,

it shook me to the core,

like the ripples on water,

when you throw stones on a river,

it was silent and serene,

until I met you,

and I knew I was home.

Home

Him

He would stare at her with those eyes,

Those beautiful eyes,

Which would haunt for days,

As if she could lose her senses.

Fall into my heart,

Before spring is over,

Melt into my heart before summer,

Sweep me off my feet,

Like autumn,

Freeze in my eyes in winter,

And stay there forever.

Sometimes I wonder where was it hiding,

All that feeling,

The feeling of sadness, the happiness, the anger,

That overwhelming feeling,

As if it was just waiting to burst,

Like a dormant volcano,

Or maybe it was waiting to be kissed,

Like a sleeping beauty,

It was feeling to be loved,

Or maybe find a way back into love.

I forgive you for the time we spent,

I forgive you for the long-lasting kisses,

I forgive you when we walked hand in hand under the night sky,

I forgive you myself for loving you more,

I forgive you for not being there for me when I needed you the most,

I forgive you because being there is what relationships are for.

Insanity

You call her Insane, since you lost your sanity,

All those prime years of youth spent loving you,

Blaming her is a brutal insanity,

She stood with you, when you didn't have clarity,

It was two-way road and you threw it away for your pride and vanity,

You killed what little love was left of her, since you are a curse on humanity.

She was always there,

In the breath you took,

In your thoughts,

When you drank coffee,

In the bed you made,

In your wandering eyes,

She was always between us,

I couldn't fill the void,

Guess she never left.

As I fall into the abyss,

All can see is the darkness,

The pain shatters my chest,

And want to burst out in tears,

The voice no one could hear,

Or harsh echoes from afar.

I am burning in the fire from the eternity.

Don't know why it doesn't engulf me.

I tired so harder to lose in flames.

But the fire inside me appears to be stronger.

It fights every day and I rise, just like a fire-breathing dragon.

Silence

She went through phases like the moon,

From the light to dark and everything in between,

To make him forget about her and so on,

She was left shattered and broken,

Now, all she could find is silence,

Who were lovers once upon.

Silence

He had turned her into a monster,

But why she was the one with blood on her hands,

He walks happily and nothing to bother,

But why she's the one with all hurt and pain,

He was just getting on her,

But she has to let go,

Otherwise, he would destroy her.

What was she hiding behind all that hurt and pain?

That she walked with all that burden an extra mile.

When they watched her cry and burn.

How long was she all broken?

Ever since they told she had beautiful smile.

He thought he could throw her around,

Like a piece of cake,

But she knew that's the only thing she wouldn't take,

She had to take the difficult step,

And then she wasn't going to stop,

After that everything was gonna change,

On that only her life would depend.

She's at peace right now,

Since she hasn't lied,

For her existence,

She remained true to herself,

And she doesn't have to prove it to anyone,

Because she sleeps like a baby now.

She is different, that's why you can't hate her,

Because she is real in the world full of fakes,

She knows how to love deeply, that is what you fear,

Hidden fear of need to be felt and embraced.

From the day she remembers, she is burning from inside.

It can be quite painful to pass each day without it crossing your mind at once.

Sometimes you gotta leave the past or it can stop or pause you from moving forward.

And she must keep it locked away, because she is the force.

I am accustomed to the blisters on my feet,

As I have walked on uneven ground,

I know how to breathe, how to stand,

Even when parts of me are sad,

I have fought the war alone you know,

And walk with pride every day,

I taught myself to grow,

As I've taught myself not to depend,

When people do all pretend,

And you don't know who is the foe or friend,

For I learned to hold my hand.

I dropped my guard for you,

Because I never felt like that for anyone else,

The moment we met I knew we are cut from the same cloth,

We wanted same things,

Because you and me made the unsolved puzzle.

I removed the mask for you,

For you to love me madly,

Because I was made of those broken pieces,

And love those parts, which you don't understand.

From the spring flowers,

to the cold winters,

Where they held hands together,

Like the raindrops falling from skies,

And those endless nights,

Their love never found home.

Gasping for air as I breathe,

All I can feel is the pain or ache,

Every cell in my body pleads,

It doesn't want to give up,

But I am tired of everything,

Because I am not good at pretending,

3

Stardust Girl

I saw him walking recklessly across the street,

So many unanswered questions in his eyes,

Apparently was in love once with a doe eyed beauty once,

There were no words left for him guess,

It couldn't hurt him anymore I bet,

His allies were the enemies in disguise,

The world we live in is a web of lies,

There was a ray of hope in him left,

For he would know he would meet someone,

Whom he doesn't have to please and wouldn't judge,

And she will be the only one.

She closed all the roads, which led toward her,

Because her heart is priceless wonder,

One day she's gonna reveal,

She says with an obnoxious smile,

If you are willing to walk an extra mile.

Bloom

She traveled through the darkness,

Trying to chase the stars,

The weight of the world was holding her down,

She was trying to keep herself awake,

Because it was the time to bloom.

Bloom

Stardust

She was made of those dreams,

which comes once in a lifetime.

She's the only one you can trust.

But was never yours to keep,

You have to time travel if you must.

She's connected with an invisible thread,

which can't be broken anytime.

Because she was made of stardust.

Stardust

It was her story now,

She against the world,

She wasn't worthy of him,

So, she had to let him go,

She would still believe in love,

But she will be bonding,

And it would be pure and simple.

A broken person cannot love,

So, I have to love myself first,

To fall in love with you,

And this time it's going to be forever.

Don't think that your emotions or pain
is any less,

It's all about how others perceive it,

They have no idea, what you have endured,

Because you're strong and haven't said a word,

There might be hundred reasons, but
they're better left unsaid.

There's a storm coming this side,

I can feel it in my bones,

The winds are changing directions,

And the overturning leaf is a sign,

There's no more room for doubt,

I can smell freedom in the air,

And I feel it is gonna stay forever.

Together we are strong they would say,

When it was always happy and gay,

The sun was bright and the summers were filled with fun,

Hardly they knew what was in store for them,

Just a fun-time activity could turn into a nightmare,

If that day one of them hadn't taken that path.

Now since you compared the relationship with furniture,

Here's a thing or two about relationships,

The one which stands or fights through toughest of time,

The chances of it lasting are longer,

Why?

It has seen bad and ugly days,

The sad and moody days,

Good and lovely days,

The days were everything felt senseless,

The days you felt lost,

The days you tried to pull each other up,

The days where you motivated each other,

And stood for each other when world was falling apart,

That kind of relationship lasts longer.

Love is a complex blend of emotions,

It's a feeling that can't be described in words,

A meeting of two souls and it's connections,

You stand like a rock when they need you,

And provide a shoulder to lean on,

Makes you kind and vulnerable,

You always put their needs before own,

One moment we are on top of the world,

And another it can bring you down on knees,

Sometimes she wonders what went wrong,

Why she was so hurt and sometimes hard on herself,

Why she had to bear the pain of someone else's wrongdoings,

The days were gloomy and the way she walked with that burdened heart,

There was something that kept them apart,

There was an invisible bonding,

But it required a lot of healing.

She had a strange feeling today,

A feeling of longing,

To look into those beautiful eyes,

That she missed each day,

It gave her a sense of belonging.

The darkness loves her,

It gives a her a glow,

When she moves through the alley,

The shadows follow,

The leaves begin to stir and

the wind to whisper,

Making her more beautiful,

like an unbeatable warrior.

It's only December my heart says,

When the cold winter breeze and misty mornings bring back those memories,

It's only January my heart says,

The winter is not over yet,

Why am I so gloomy and we haven't met,

It's only February my heart says,

How long would be the wait,

Because spring hasn't arrived yet,

I want to watch the flowers bloom again,

And the trees transform,

When the Sun will shine bright and skies are blue,

When spring arrives, the air is warm,

Bringing new beginnings and life to the heart,

The wind will blow gently and it's a warm hue,

We meet this time and nothing can keep us apart.

There's a longing to meet, since the day she saw him,

As if they were meant for each other,

They had that love in their eyes,

That unfinished love,

Will they meet every again,

That only the time would say,

If it is meant to be, it will be.

She wished she could believe everything,

But there was puzzle that was missing,

Something wasn't fitting,

Because she chose to ignore the instinct,

But now everything was clear,

And nothing made more sense than ever.

We might be different,

You and me, but what makes us glued,

Together might be the passion for love,

That intimacy without any physical connection,

Where we talk to each other in dreams,

And we know that we are connected in some way or the another,

Maybe in we were bound for eternity,

That we keep bumping to each other,

In all the lives,

That thread which joins us together,

We are meant to meet every time,

As if it is a serendipity.

Love shouldn't be complicated,

It should be like a walk in the park,

It shouldn't come with rules of do's and don'ts,

Ten I would say that it is not love and it should be given one last thought,

If you can't be yourself with the one you love,

Then it is time to move,

It should be pure innocence and lot of time spending with each other,

Because love is something that is meant to stay forever.

4

For You

Hearts here,

Hearts there,

Chaos everywhere,

Don't need those rose-tinted glasses,

But an extra pair of eyes,

That can read and set the soul on fire.

Here I was standing under the fountain of youth,

Thinking that we always stay young,

Do we always?

Yes, we can at heart,

Playful and never a moment idle,

You see me I am always on the move,

But there are times where I feel

My body says you need to stop,

I pause for a bit and relax,

And gather all the inner strength,

As that's what keeps me alive,

And everyday I feel grateful,

Knowing that we must leave some day,

And that's the hardest truth.

Care

It going to be you and only you forever,

So be gentle to your heart,

Be gentle to you.

Care

Do you feel stuck in an infinity?

As if there's no way out,

You get overwhelmed,

And there's no one around,

You are so broken and damaged,

But don't how to respond.

Life begins with a small hint of seed,

Uncertainity of how it might be,

But that's the way of nature indeed.

There's always an end to the sadness,

Finding someone who loves your madness,

Who loves you to the core,

Even when you are lost in the darkness.

That's the beauty of life.

We can choose to close the door,

or leave the door open.

We can choose to leave the table that

doesn't serve us and move on.

We can always choose new paths and possibilities,

And go in search of what we really want.

From the death's grasp she rose,

With heart full of hope,

Past is a memory to keep,

A guide to keep her future steep,

The sun will shine and the flowers bloom,

She will find a way out of the gloom,

The second chance to live and learn,

Spreading her wings to fly again.

To love someone, when they are broken,

And to know what it feels like,

To be left in the darkness alone,

But it's a very brave, to let someone go,

When they love you, or whether you love them so much,

Because you don't want to hurt them.

The nature has its own ways of adapting,

What we think as simple might be quite complicated,

Each tiny living thing in this universe is linked to you,

If you speak to them, they will respond,

Your mind is a powerful thing,

Like the smell of grass, flower, tree, wind, earth,

Everything remains in our subconscious mind,

But when the time and place is right,

It would try and link to get back to you,

The more you give to nature, it will give back.

Things you don't want to remember are hard to forget,

Those times are difficult,

Sometimes you ever wonder if you could become a ghost,

It would make things easier,

If you could disappear in thin air.

That's the thing about belief,

It makes you imagine impossible,

Achieve the impossible,

The stronger your belief is, clearer the path becomes,

And you stop worrying about outcomes.

Sometimes it crawls upon you,

That feeling of uneasiness,

The demons of the past,

It feels like choking,

But you had to let go,

Even though it seems hard,

You fought out bravely.

The arrival of instinct,

Is so much interesting

That you are so closer to it,

But you seem to be so ignorant,

It keeps giving you signs,

You walk right over the warnings,

There's so much to learn,

Face it so that, when it's your turn,

Walk over it and claim your winnings.

Illusions are tricks of nature,

And its nothing but a lie,

They dance before your eyes,

Like a mirage and tricks of light,

Creating visions that fade away.

We see what we want to see,

And believe what we want to believe,

But the truth is not what it seems,

Our thoughts and feeling can deceive.

We chase after what we can't have,

A dream that slips through our grasp.

And the reality can be bitter,

The sooner we know the better,

Illusions may be shimmering and bright,

But the truth always comes to the light.

Amongst those abandoned paths,

are lost the voice of those,

silent wails which were never heard,

as they remained lost in the darkness.

The ones who needed love.

The ones who wanted to be protected.

Remained buried and now remain,

in our dreams and prayers.

Heal

Like a soft summer storm,

And a gentle drop of grace,

It comes in many forms,

And flows like a river wild,

Craving path though pain and smiles,

Bringing life to barren lands,

Full of twists and turns,

And highs and lows,

To rise above all and find the strength,

A journey to healing.

Heal

You wished to chase time and hold it forever,

But can't think anytime was memorable,

Letting it go was the best thing ever,

Everything was one way as she remembers,

It was the time to disappear.

What lies beneath the chambers,

The truth which was lost somewhere,

Either burnt to ashes or lost in the sea,

Shadowed secrets that lie in the grave,

They are the precious of all,

Who gave their life and lost blood,

In the pursuit of happiness and survival,

The most valued treasure of nature,

And cannot be traded for any valuable thing in the world,

The life of the one true love.

Love is the most beautiful and
the deadliest thing in the world.
Its like jumping in the fire.
If you come out unburnt then you
are the luckiest.
If burnt, then the scars remain.
And you emerge out from the ashes
Like a fire-breathing dragon.

A new beginning from ashes to life,

A chance to grow and heal the heart,

A path to the future filled with hope,

Where dreams come true, in the morning light.

Like a phoenix rising from ashes of past,

Embracing change and overcomes hardships,

Those once took their toll,

With renewed strength it reclaims the soul.

Brave are those who wear heart on their sleeves every day,

It's not so easy to put up a smile each day with courage,

Wake up with energy and walk with head held high,

And face the challenges life throws each day.

Forgotten are those,

whose silent wails were hidden in the

darkness of the nights passed,

All around were the echoes of the sadness,

And lay numb in those terrorized paths,

Waiting for the forests to bloom and,

to be reborn from the ashes one day.

You don't need too much time to read someone,

It's all about experience,

The person who loves you would not play mind games,

It's plain and simple.

Unknow is the path which lies ahead,

Like a sword hanging above the head,

If there was a time machine made,

And could tour around everything,

Not knowing what would you change,

Unable to recollect what you had lost,

Because the world you live in is an illusion,

Like a mirage in a faraway desert.

Fragile Silence

In the fragile silences of wintery night,

With still air and the frozen trees around,

The white velvety snow beneath my feet,

I feel the darkness wraps me tight,

The warmth of the fire keeps me alive.

Fragile Silence

I look up and the Moon is in full glow,

Like a silver sphere in the night sky,

It's like a magic of nature I know.

The trees whisper the secrets of life,

With a world filled with dreams and desire,

To pause and breath and to be still.

To jump into the fire,

For the forbidden love,

To walk in those dark paths,

And to lose your calm,

Like a raging bull.

It's commendable,

That you put so much effort put a smile,

When you are burning inside,

And sail through smoothly with life,

Refuse to Descend

Everyone is fighting a different battle,

The one we don't know,

Some we might know,

The hardest part is realizing that

You have your own demons to fight,

But that should not involve someone,

Never drown others in order to stay afloat,

Then you're just like everyone,

Instead learn how can be useful to each other,

And work towards the goal,

When one begins to drift away,

Be an anchor to them.

It's the season of death,

Losing near and dear ones,

The recent days have been hard,

It has shaken faith,

We might see someone smiling,

Tomorrow, we might not see them,

We must be ready for the calling,

The broke they leave can't be filled,

As if time has come to a standstill,

Some would go on, but some are left with darkness,

It might be crawling upon you,

And the never-ending loneliness,

Only thing is to live the moment,

Before the clock starts ticking.

How strong is the human heart,

Which heals so soon,

Every time it breaks apart.

You don't know how it feels,

To be broken,

To be burned inside,

To maintain your sanity,

You don't know how to heal,

Because everyone thinks you're insane.

Negative People

Always like to be around positive people

They draw out positive vibes or energy from positive people for their advantage,

They can't or don't know how to control their mind,

They always look for advice from others,

They suck out all the happiness because they are unhappy,

Can't make up their mind on what they want, don't succeed and don't allow others too,

Always look for inspiration from others and try to mimic them, as they don't have identity,

Walk away from negative energies and see the change.

Like a sword hanging above the head

If there was a time machine, and could

turn around everything,

Unknown is the path which lies ahead,

Not knowing what to change,

Unable to recollect what you had lost,

The world you live in is an illusion,

Like a mirage in the desert.

Liars have no conscience,

They lie like it's a daily dose of vitamin,

And lie to people for fun,

Liars kill already dead, and then kill lying,

Before leaving them dead.

The war you're fighting,

You're not alone in this,

Others too are suffering,

Some won't tell, some won't show,

But there's only one thing you need to know,

Stand firm on your ground,

No matter what comes,

Because there's aways a silver lining.

Scars Speak

Let the scars speak for you,

How beautiful you are,

Adore all the flaws and love them,

With each passing day,

Each one would tell a different story,

That how you survived the pain,

And emerged so beautifully,

Leaving behind the cocoon.

Scars Speak

5

Mirabilia

You refuse to sulk, and look at the day as a new beginning waiting for miracles to happen. You refuse to give up, because the life has given noting and has taken more and more from you and left empty handed. You refuse to descend and swim above those dark waters fighting the demons who eat your soul every day.

www.ingramcontent.com/pod-product-compliance
Lightning Source LLC
LaVergne TN
LVHW070938070526
838199LV00035B/647